THE TOILET ROLL ACTIVITY BOOK

Models by Melanie Grimshaw-Smith

Illustrations by John Bigwood
Photography by Andrew Pickford
Written and edited by Lauren Farnsworth
Designed by Zoe Bradley
Cover design by Angie Allison

Buster Books

CONTENTS

It's easy to follow the step-by-step instructions in this book to make creative projects with toilet-roll tubes. At the back of the book you will find a materials check list which contains all the basic materials you will need.

Some projects are easy and others are more tricky. To help you decide what to make, each project has been given a star rating that tells you its difficulty level. Just read the star-rating guide below.

Toilet-roll tubes come in lots of different sizes, and any size can be used to achieve great results. However, if a project makes use of more than one tube it's best if all of them are the same size.

Some projects may use sharp objects, such as scissors, staples or safety pins. Always ask an adult before using anything sharp, just in case you need any help.

STAR-RATING GUIDE
Easy peasy ☆   Pretty simple ☆ ☆

Getting tricky ☆ ☆ ☆   Project master ☆ ☆ ☆ ☆

OLI THE OWL

Have a hoot making Oli the owl ... and then create a whole nest of feathery friends if you fancy.

TO MAKE ONE OWL YOU WILL NEED:
1 toilet-roll tube
1 sheet of A4 paper, coloured or patterned
Pencil
Scissors
Black felt-tip pen
Sticky tape

1. Place the toilet-roll tube so that the bottom of it lines up with the bottom of the piece of paper.

3. To make the paper the right length, wrap it around your tube and make a mark so that the two edges overlap by 2 cm. Cut along in a line from this point.

2. Use a pencil to mark where the top of the tube comes to. Fold the piece of paper at this point and cut along the fold. The paper will now be the same height as the tube.

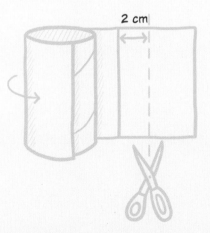

2 cm

5

4. Wrap the paper around the tube. Hold it in place with one hand and use the other hand to push the front edge of the tube inwards to the centre of the tube to create a semi-circle shape. Do the same with the back edge of the roll. This will form the owl's ears.

5. Lay the paper flat again and draw your owl design. Use the semi-circle imprint as a guide to show where to position your drawing. You could use one of the designs from the owls on the previous page or create your own.

6. Finally wrap the paper around the tube. Make sure your owl design lines up with the ears and secure with sticky tape. Fold the front and the back of the paper inwards so they meet in the middle with the already-folded cardboard and form the ears.

YOU CAN DRAW DIRECTLY ON TO THE TOILET-ROLL TUBE INSTEAD OF WRAPPING IT IN PAPER, IF YOU PREFER.

PERFECT POTS

Create the perfect place to keep your pencils.

TO MAKE ONE PENCIL POT YOU WILL NEED:

1 toilet-roll tube

Masking tape

Double-sided sticky tape

A circle of card, the same circumference as the toilet-roll tube

Scissors

Ribbons of different colours, patterns and widths

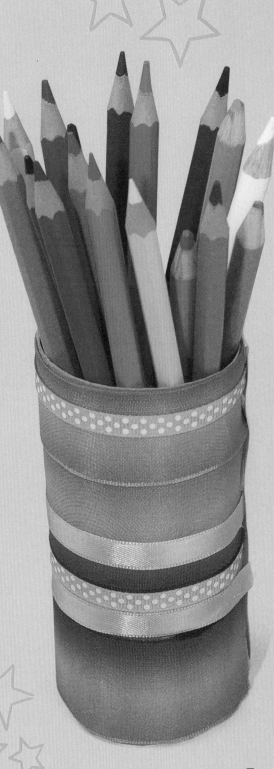

1. Cover one end of the toilet-roll tube with strips of masking tape.

3. Cut lengths of different types of ribbon, all the same circumference as the tube. You will need around 12 lengths, depending on how wide your ribbons are.

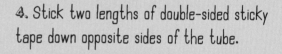

2. Using double-sided sticky tape, stick the circle of card to the masking-taped end of the tube.

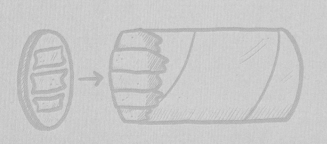

4. Stick two lengths of double-sided sticky tape down opposite sides of the tube.

5. One at a time, wrap each ribbon around the circumference of the tube, securing it to the double-sided sticky tape. Make sure the ribbon ends all meet in the same place.

YOU COULD MAKE A DIFFERENT COLOUR PENCIL POT FOR EACH DIFFERENT-COLOURED SET OF PENS AND PENCILS.

6. To hide the row of ribbon ends, stick a length of ribbon over them, using double-sided sticky tape to secure it. Fold the end of this piece of ribbon down the top end.

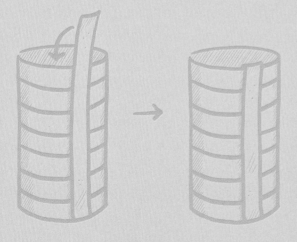

ROCKING ROCKETS

These colourful rockets really do look like they are zooming into space.

TO MAKE ONE ROCKET YOU WILL NEED:

1 toilet-roll tube

Patterned paper

Sticky tape

Scissors

Coloured card

Compass and pencil

Double-sided sticky tape

Length of string, about 30 cm long

PVA glue

Assorted ribbon

1. Cover the toilet-roll tube by rolling it in the patterned paper and securing the paper with sticky tape. Trim the paper to size with scissors if needed.

2. To make the top of the rocket, cut a circle of coloured card about 10 cm in diameter.

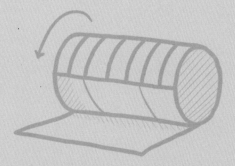

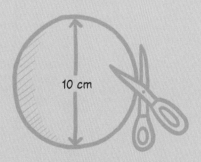

10 cm

USING WIGGLY RIBBONS FOR THE
ROCKET'S TAIL REALLY MAKES IT
LOOK LIKE IT'S FLYING.

3. Using a pencil, lightly divide the circle into three equal-sized sections. Cut one of these sections out from the circle.

4. Curve the circle piece into a cone shape and secure with sticky tape.

5. Take the piece of string and tie a large knot in one end, then thread the other end through the top of the cone from the underside. If there isn't a space big enough for you to thread the string through, then you can make one by gently poking through with the tip of a pencil.

7. To make the tail of your rocket, cut the ribbon into about six 15 cm-long pieces.

6. Glue the cone to the top of the toilet-roll tube.

8. Tape the lengths of ribbon around the bottom inside edge of the tube.

OH MY, MUMMIES!

Spooky times. Pop these cute mummies around your room for Halloween.

TO MAKE ONE MUMMY YOU WILL NEED:

A pair of stick-on googly eyes
1 toilet-roll tube
PVA glue
Toilet paper
Fabric strips
String
Scissors

1. Stick the googly eyes on to the tube, between halfway and two-thirds up.

14

3. Wrap the fabric strips and string around the tube to create different textures.

YOU CAN USE DIFFERENT COLOURS OF TISSUE PAPER, FABRIC AND STRING TO CREATE MULTICOLOURED MUMMIES.

2. Take a length of toilet paper and wrap it loosely around the tube, leaving a gap where the eyes are placed. Secure each end of the toilet paper with a blob of glue.

BIRD FEEDER

This sticky, tasty bird feeder will bring feathered friends straight to your garden for a well-deserved treat.

TO MAKE ONE BIRD FEEDER YOU WILL NEED:

1 toilet-roll tube

Peanut butter

Teaspoon

Bird seed

Plate

String

Scissors

1. Coat the outer surface of a toilet-roll tube in a layer of peanut butter. Why not get sticky and use your fingers to spread it? Alternatively, a teaspoon will do the trick.

PLEASE NOTE:
THIS PROJECT USES A FOOD THAT CONTAINS NUTS, SO TAKE CARE IF YOU HAVE A NUT ALLERGY.

PEANUT BUTTER

2. Pour some bird seed on to a plate and roll the buttery tube in the seeds until it is covered all over.

3. Thread a length of string through the tube so you can hang your bird feeder outdoors.

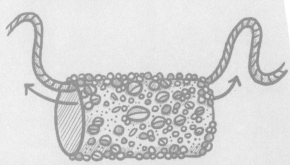

IF YOU DON'T HAVE A GARDEN, YOU CAN HANG THE BIRD FEEDER OUTSIDE YOUR WINDOW.

CACTUS FLOWERS

These beautiful flowers are easier to make than they look. Display them on a sunny windowsill.

TO MAKE ONE SIMPLE FLOWER YOU WILL NEED:
1 toilet-roll tube
Scissors
Pencil

TO MAKE ONE COMPLEX FLOWER YOU WILL NEED:
1 toilet-roll tube
Scissors
Pencil
PVA glue
Clothes pegs

Simple flower

1. Cut 1 cm-wide strips up to just over halfway along the length of the toilet-roll tube.

2. Snip the ends of each strip into small points.

3. Curl each strip outwards by wrapping it around a pencil.

4. At the other end of the tube, cut triangular points around the rim, to about a third of the way down.

5. Using your fingers, curl the triangular points inwards. Gently squash the tube down with your hand so it sits flatter.

IT'S EASY TO EXPERIMENT WITH THESE FLOWERS - CHANGE THE WIDTH OF THE STRIPS OR CURL THEM INWARDS OR OUTWARDS TO CREATE DIFFERENT EFFECTS.

Complex flower

1. Cut the toilet-roll tube at a point approximately one third of its length, leaving the other piece two thirds the length.

2. Take the larger section and cut it lengthways into 1.5 cm-wide strips, stopping about 1 cm from the bottom.

3. Curl each strip outwards by wrapping it around a pencil. Stand the toilet-roll tube up on its uncut end.

4. Take the smaller section of tube and cut it open lengthways.

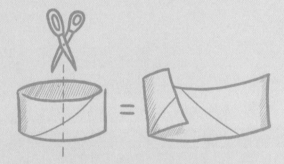

5. Cut it into 0.5 cm-wide strips, almost to the bottom.

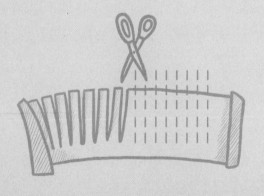

6. Curl it around so it is in a double loop.

7. Using your fingers or a pencil, curl all the strips outwards.

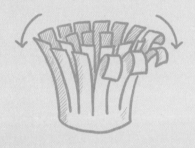

8. Glue this loop inside the bigger section of toilet-roll tube. You can use clothes pegs to hold the pieces together while the glue dries.

WOOLLY SHEEP

Baaaa! This cute sheep is almost as woolly as a real one.

TO MAKE ONE SHEEP YOU WILL NEED:

1 toilet-roll tube

Scissors

White and cream wool

PVA glue

Pencil

Sequins

23

1. To make the body of the sheep, flatten the toilet-roll tube, then cut off two rings, both 0.5 cm in width.

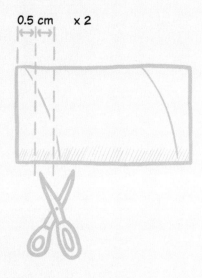

3. Wrap the wool around the rim of the circle until it's well padded, and the tube is completely covered. Secure the ends of the wool with glue.

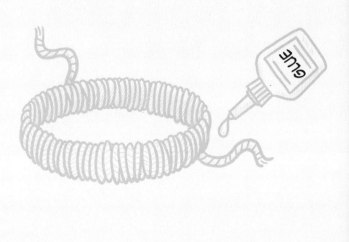

2. Make a cut in both of them to break the circle and open them out. Tape the two pieces together to make a bigger circle.

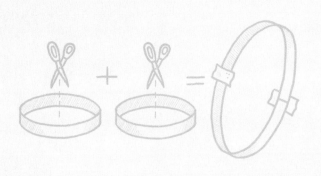

4. To make a tail for the sheep's body, take three lengths of wool, about 6 cm long, plait them together and make a small loop. Secure this loop to the body with glue.

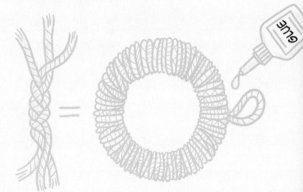

5. To make the sheep's legs, cut a 3 cm-wide ring of toilet-roll tube, flatten it, and make three triangular cuts, about 1 cm apart. Make the middle triangle slightly bigger than the two either side.

7. Cut open the last ring of the tube and flatten it out. Draw a sheep's head shape on the cardboard and cut this out. Glue on small sequins for the eyes, and attach the head to the body with glue.

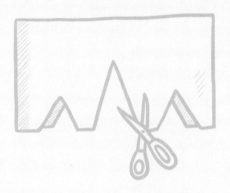

6. Open out the ring and sit the sheep's body on top. Secure the pieces together with glue.

YOU CAN USE DIFFERENT COLOURS OF WOOL TO MAKE A RAINBOW-COLOURED FLOCK OF SHEEP.

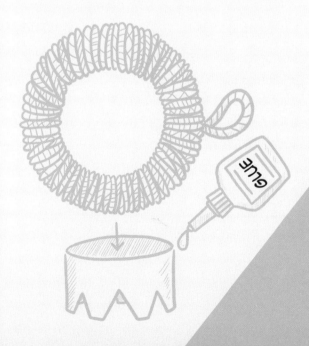

25

LITTLE STARS

Be the star of the show by creating these tiny twinklers.

TO MAKE ONE STAR YOU WILL NEED:

Paint
Paintbrush
1 toilet-roll tube
Scissors
Double-sided sticky tape
Coloured paper
Length of thin ribbon or string,
    about 20 cm

1. Paint a toilet-roll tube in a bright colour on the inside only and leave to dry completely. Once dry, cut three 1 cm-wide rings from the toilet-roll tube.

1 cm x 3

2. Stick the three pieces together in a crisscross shape, slotting them inside each other and securing with double-sided sticky tape.

3. Cut the coloured paper into 1 cm squares, and use these to decorate your star in any pattern you want. Secure the paper squares with double-sided sticky tape.

4. To hang your star, loop the length of ribbon around one of the arms of the star and secure with a knot.

1 cm

ADD SEQUINS OR GLITTER TO MAKE YOUR STARS SPARKLE.

RACE CARS

These little vehicles are based on classic racing cars.

TO MAKE ONE CAR YOU WILL NEED:

Paint in assorted colours
Paintbrush
1 toilet-roll tube
Black felt-tip pen
Scissors
PVA glue
4 black or grey buttons of similar size

1. Paint the toilet-roll tube in one colour on the outside only, and leave to dry completely. Once dry, paint on details, such as racing stripes and a circle. Once the paint is completely dry, write a racing number in the circle with a black felt-tip pen.

2. Squash the tube down slightly so it is an oval shape.

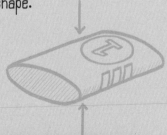

3. On top of the tube, behind the racing number, cut two parallel slits going lengthways, then another horizontal slit to join them, making an 'H' shape.

4. This should make two flaps. Bend the front flap up to make a windscreen and fold the back flap down to make a seat.

5. Glue the four buttons to the sides of the toilet-roll tube, two at the front and two at the back to make the wheels.

IF YOU HAVE A FAVOURITE RACING TEAM, PAINT YOUR CAR IN ITS COLOURS.

FLYING FISH

The colourful tails of these fish will ripple in the wind.

TO MAKE ONE FISH YOU WILL NEED:
Coloured tissue paper
Scissors
1 toilet-roll tube
PVA glue
Ribbon
2 ring-hole stickers
2 sequins
A length of string, about 30 cm

1. From the coloured tissue paper, cut enough semi-circular scale shapes to cover one toilet-roll tube. They should be about 2.5 cm long in size.

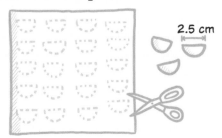

2.5 cm

2. Glue the scale shapes to the tube to cover it completely and so that they overlap each other like real scales.

3. Cut six strips of tissue paper, each 1 cm wide and 15 cm long. Also cut six lengths of ribbon, about 15 cm long.

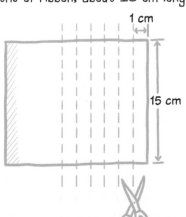

1 cm

15 cm

4. Glue the strips of tissue and ribbon around the bottom inside edge of tube.

5. Add eyes to the fish by sticking two ring-hole stickers on opposite sides of the top of the tube. Glue sequins to the middle of the ring-hole stickers.

6. Using scissors, make two small holes at the top of the tube, about 0.5 cm from the edge. Make sure these holes aren't close to the fish's eyes. Tie a loop of string through the holes, so you can hang up your fish.

WHY NOT TRY HOLOGRAPHIC PAPER TO GIVE YOUR FISH SUPER-SPARKLY SCALES?

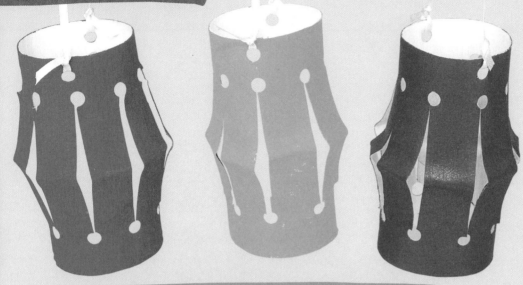

LOVELY LANTERNS

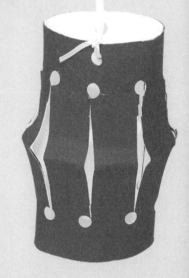

Brighten up any room with these colourful hanging lanterns.

TO MAKE ONE LANTERN YOU WILL NEED:

Paint

Paintbrush

1 toilet-roll tube

Hole punch, small enough to fit inside the toilet-roll tube

Scissors

Length of thin ribbon or string, about 30 cm

33

STRING UP YOUR LANTERNS WITH FAIRY LIGHTS TO MAKE THEM LOOK LIKE THEY ARE REALLY GLOWING.

1. Paint the toilet-roll tube one colour on the outside and another on the inside. Leave to dry completely.

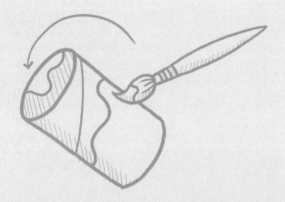

2. Once dry, use a hole punch to create eight holes in a ring around each end of the tube, about 3 cm from the edges. Make sure each top and bottom hole are aligned with each other.

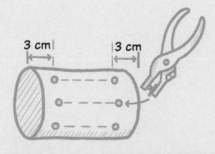

3. Using scissors, cut slits lengthways between each of the top and bottom holes.

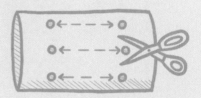

4. Using your thumb and forefinger, pinch a horizontal fold halfway down each of the strips that are created by the slits. Gently squash the lantern at both ends to make the folds bulge out around the middle.

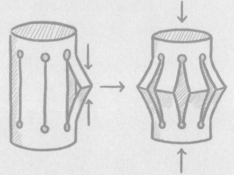

5. At the top of the lantern, punch two holes at opposite sides, about 0.5 cm from the edge. Tie a loop of ribbon through the holes so you can hang up the lantern.

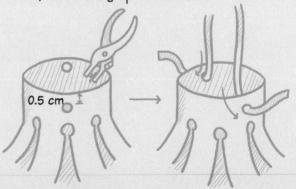

34

TIDY BOX

Get crafty and organise your desk all at the same time.

TO MAKE ONE TIDY BOX YOU WILL NEED:

1 shoe box, about 12 cm x 20 cm in size
Colourful wrapping paper
Scissors
Sticky tape
10 toilet-roll tubes

1. Wrap the shoe box in the wrapping paper, exactly how you would wrap a present, except leaving the top open. Secure the edges with sticky tape to give it a neat finish.

2. Check the toilet-roll tubes are the same height as the shoe box, trimming them at the end if you need to.

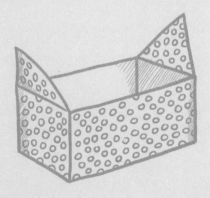

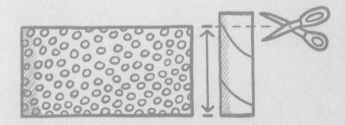

3. Slot the toilet-roll tubes into the shoe box, so they fit into two rows.

YOU CAN USE A BIGGER SHOE BOX AND MORE TOILET-ROLL TUBES IF YOU HAVE A LOT OF STUFF TO ORGANISE.

APPLE AND PUMPKIN

These cute decorations are perfect for autumn or Halloween.

TO MAKE ONE APPLE YOU WILL NEED:

A4 green plain or patterned card or paper

Scissors

2 toilet-roll tubes

Green paint

Paintbrush

Double-sided sticky tape

PVA glue

Small twig, about 7 cm long

1. Holding the green card or paper widthways, cut it into 2 cm-wide strips. An A4 sheet of paper should make about 15 strips.

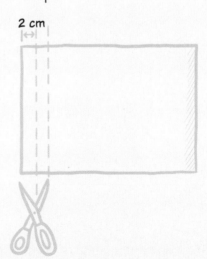

2 cm

2. Paint one toilet-roll tube green on the outside.

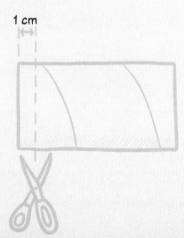

3. Take the other toilet-roll tube and cut off a 1 cm-wide ring. Paint this green and leave it to dry completely.

1 cm

4. Pinch folds at opposite ends of the green ring to make it into a leaf shape.

5. Attach small strips of double-sided sticky tape to both ends of each strip of green card.

6. Take one strip of green card and stick the end inside the top of the green toilet-roll tube. Curve the strip into a semi-circle shape and stick the other end inside the bottom of the tube.

7. Repeat the previous step with all the green card strips, spacing them evenly around the tube into a ball-like shape. It's okay if the strips overlap each other a little.

8. Finish the apple by gluing the green leaf shape to the top end of one of the green strips, and gluing the small twig just inside the top of the tube.

TO MAKE A PUMPKIN, USE ORANGE CARD INSTEAD OF GREEN, AND PAINT THE INNER TOILET-ROLL TUBE ORANGE.

MINI GIFT BOX

Perfect to pack little presents.

1. Cut a rectangle of wrapping paper the same length as the toilet-roll tube, and wide enough to wrap around the whole tube.

TO MAKE ONE GIFT BOX YOU WILL NEED:

Colourful wrapping paper

Scissors

1 toilet-roll tube

Double-sided sticky tape

Ribbon or twine

2. Stick double-sided sticky tape around the complete circumference of the tube, at both ends and in the middle. Roll the tube in the wrapping paper, so it is completely covered and secured firmly to the double-sided sticky tape.

4. Close one end of the tube by folding the arches inwards over each other. Insert a small gift into the tube at the open end, and then close this end in the same way.

3. Flatten the tube with your hands and cut both ends into curved arches.

5. Cut a length of ribbon or twine, about four times the length of your gift box, and tie this around the box, securing with a bow. Cut off the ends of the bow if they are too long.

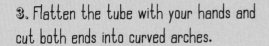

SMALL SWEETS ARE THE PERFECT SIZE TO FIT INSIDE THESE LITTLE BOXES.

FLOWER POWER

Unleash some flower power with this pretty wall hanging. Make a field full or go mad with colour – it's up to you.

TO MAKE ONE LARGE FLOWER YOU WILL NEED:

10 toilet-roll tubes

Paint, in 2 or more colours

Paintbrush

Scissors

Double-sided sticky tape

Length of thin ribbon or string, about 30 cm

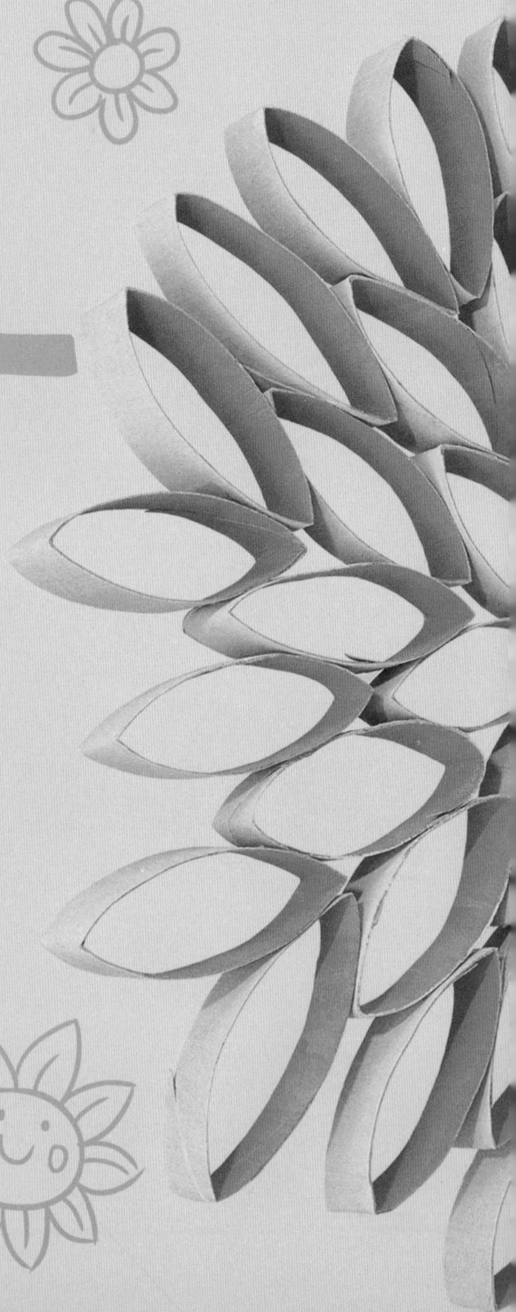

1. Choose at least two colours and paint all ten toilet-roll tubes one colour on the outside and another colour on the inside. Let the first coat dry, then give them one more coat of paint.

2. When the paint is completely dry, use scissors to cut each tube into five equal-sized rings.

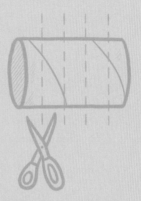

3. Pinch folds on opposite sides of each ring to create a petal shape.

4. Create a circle of eight petals by using small squares of double-sided sticky tape to secure the petals together.

43

5. Add another row of petals by sticking two petals between each pair.

7. To hang your flower, loop a 30 cm-long piece of ribbon or string through one of the outer petals and secure it with a knot.

6. Continue adding rows to make your flower larger.

TRY ARRANGING THE PETALS IN DIFFERENT PATTERNS SO YOU CAN MAKE OTHER KINDS OF FLOWERS

SPIRAL SNAKE

This slithering friend is sssss-super cool.

TO MAKE ONE SNAKE YOU WILL NEED:

Bubble wrap

Scissors

Paints

Paintbrush

1 toilet-roll tube

White paper or card

Black beads

PVA glue

1. Cut a square of bubble wrap to the same length as the toilet-roll tube. Lay the bubble wrap flat and coat the top with a layer of paint.

3. Cut the toilet-roll tube diagonally, from the top of one side and all the way round to the bottom of the other side.

2. Before the paint dries, roll the tube over the surface, so the bubble-wrap pattern prints on the tube. Leave the bubble wrap and tube to dry completely. Repeat this step using a different colour paint, layering the second colour on top of the first. Leave the tube to dry completely.

4. Do this again, starting at the same point as the first cut, but getting increasingly larger so that you end about 5 cm away from the other bottom cut. This should leave a spiral piece of tube. Put the leftover piece of toilet-roll tube aside.

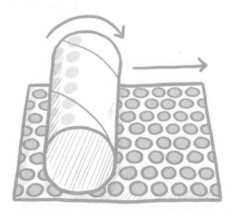

5 cm

5. At the larger end, cut the toilet-roll tube into a snake's head shape.

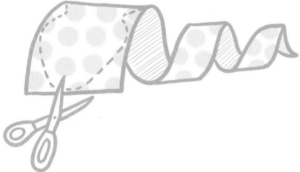

6. To add detail to the snake's head, cut out two 1 cm-long teardrop shapes from the white paper or card. Cut out two slightly smaller teardrop shapes and a forked snake-tongue shape from the piece of leftover toilet-roll tube.

1 cm

7. Glue the larger teardrop pieces to the head, and then glue the smaller teardrop pieces on top of the larger ones. Finally, glue the bead eyes between the teardrop shapes and the tongue to the end of the snake's nose.

USE A KITCHEN-ROLL TUBE TO MAKE AN EXTRA LONG, SUPER-SPIRAL SNAKE.

CURLY OCTOPUS

The perfect little eight-legged buddy.

TO MAKE ONE OCTOPUS YOU WILL NEED:

1 toilet-roll tube
Scissors
Pencil
Paints
Paintbrush
Ring-hole stickers
Colourful beads
Sequins
PVA glue

1. Choose two different colours and paint the toilet-roll tube one colour on the outside and another colour on the inside. Leave it to dry completely.

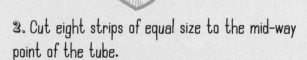

2. Cut eight strips of equal size to the mid-way point of the tube.

3. Curl each strip by wrapping it around the middle of a pencil and curling it outwards. Curl all the strips evenly, so the octopus sits down on them.

4. Stick a ring-hole sticker on the outside end of one of the tentacle strips. Choose a third colour and paint over the ring-hole sticker.

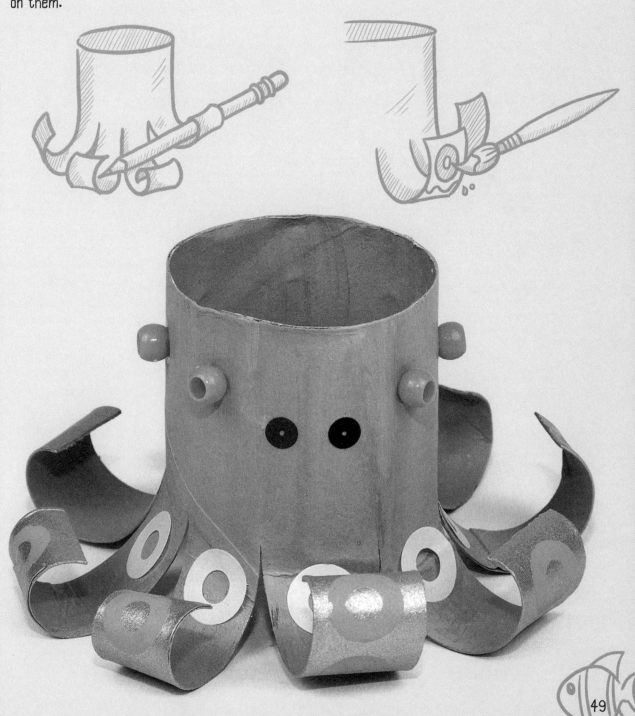

49

5. Once the paint is dry, peel off the ring-hole sticker to reveal a sucker pattern.

6. Repeat steps 4 and 5 on each tentacle strip.

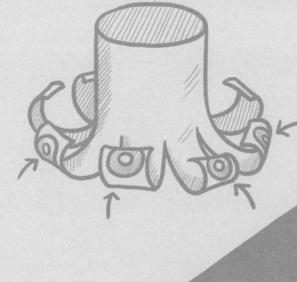

7. Decorate your octopus by sticking on more ring-hole stickers, gluing on beads, and gluing on sequins for its eyes.

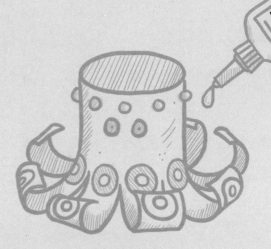

MAKE A WHOLE GANG OF OCTOPUSES IN DIFFERENT COLOURS.

CRACKING CRACKERS

Perfect for a party table, hide presents inside these cool crackers.

TO MAKE ONE CRACKER YOU WILL NEED:

A small present that will fit inside a
  toilet-roll tube, such as sweets
1 toilet-roll tube
Coloured tissue paper
Sticky tape
Wool, ribbon or string
Patterned wrapping paper

1. Put your present inside the toilet-roll tube.

2. Wrap the tube in the tissue paper, leaving an extra 6 cm of tissue paper beyond the tube at each end, and secure it with a piece of sticky tape.

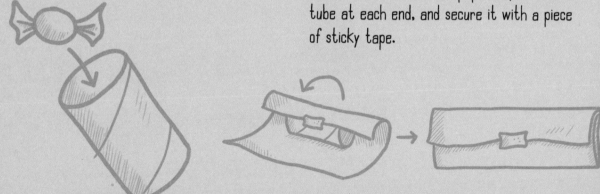

3. Gather both ends of the tissue paper by tying a length of wool, string or ribbon around them, and securing in a knot or bow.

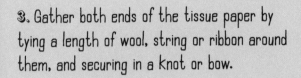

REMEMBER, THESE CRACKERS CAN'T BE PULLED OPEN LIKE SHOP-BOUGHT CRACKERS. OPEN THEM AT ONE END BY UNTYING THE STRING OR TEARING THE PAPER.

4. Wrap a rectangle of wrapping paper around the middle of the cracker, making sure it is shorter than the length of the toilet-roll tube. Secure with sticky tape.

COOL CUFFS

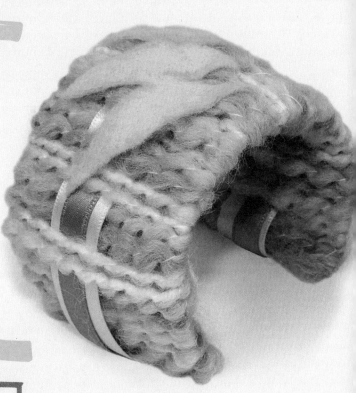

Make a pretty bracelet or a superhero cuff.

TO MAKE ONE CUFF YOU WILL NEED:

1 toilet-roll tube
Scissors
Double-sided sticky tape
Coloured wool
Coloured ribbon
Pencil
Coloured felt

1. Cut a toilet-roll tube in half, and make a cut in one piece along the length.

2. To secure the wool to the tube, stick a length of double-sided sticky tape at each cut end of the tube.

4. To add extra colour, take the ribbon and weave it under and over the lengths of wool in a strip around the cuff. Secure the ends at the back with glue.

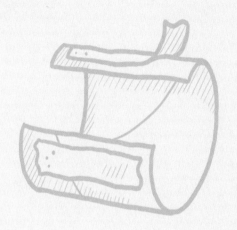

3. As neatly as you can, wrap the wool around the cuff from top to bottom. Secure the ends with a little glue.

5. To make a motif to decorate, draw a picture of your choice on to the felt. It could be a heart or a lightning bolt, for example.

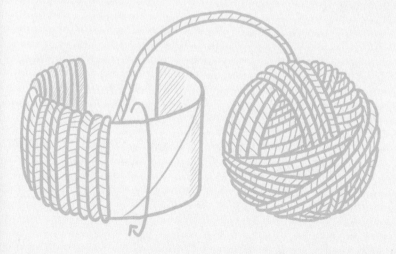

6. Cut out the motif and secure it to the front of your cuff with glue.

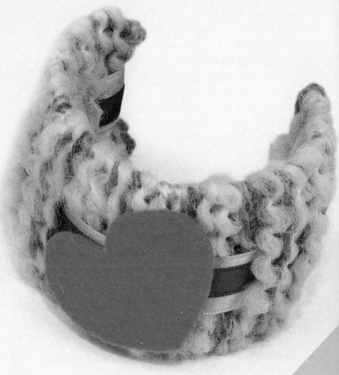

7. If your cuff is too loose, tie a piece of wool to each end by knotting it to the wool covering. Use the wool to tie the ends closer together.

YOU COULD USE THESE CUFFS FOR SUPERHERO FANCY DRESS.

BEAUTIFUL BASKET

This tiny basket can make a really sweet present.

TO MAKE ONE BASKET YOU WILL NEED:
2 toilet-roll tubes
Scissors
Pencil
Ruler
Colourful ribbon
PVA glue
2 paper fasteners

1. Cut one toilet-roll tube down one side and open it out into a rectangle.

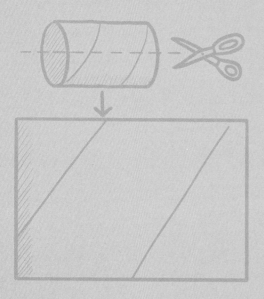

3. Cut triangles, with points facing outwards, on to the outer middle sections, on the longer sides of the rectangle as shown below.

2. Using a pencil and ruler, divide the rectangle lengthways into three equal parts. Then do the same widthways.

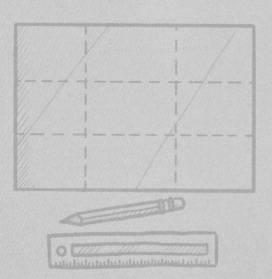

4. On each of the four outer corner sections, next to the triangles, cut three equal-sized strips, stopping at the mid-section line.

5. At each edge of the rectangle, glue a length of ribbon about 0.5 cm from the edge.

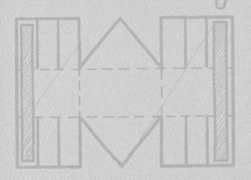

6. Gather the six strips together behind the point of the triangle, folding the rectangle round into the basket shape to achieve this. Keep the ribbon on the outside.

7. To fasten all the pieces together, push a paper fastener through the cardboard, one layer at a time, and secure it at the back.

8. To make the handle, cut a strip from your second toilet-roll tube. Glue a length of ribbon down the middle.

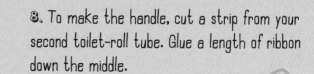

FILLED WITH SWEET-SMELLING FLOWERS, THIS MAKES THE PERFECT MOTHER'S DAY GIFT.

9. To secure the handle to the basket, reopen the paper fasteners on the inside of the basket and push them through each end of the handle. Re-fasten each of the paper fasteners.

PICTURE PERFECT

The number of arrangements you can make to create special pictures is endless.

1. Paint all five toilet-roll tubes white, inside and out. Allow them to dry completely, and then cut each tube into five equal-sized rings.

TO MAKE ONE PICTURE YOU WILL NEED:

5 toilet-roll tubes
Paints, including white
Paintbrush
Scissors
Foam board square, about 26 cm x 26 cm
Pencil
PVA glue

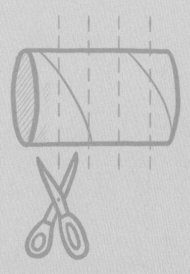

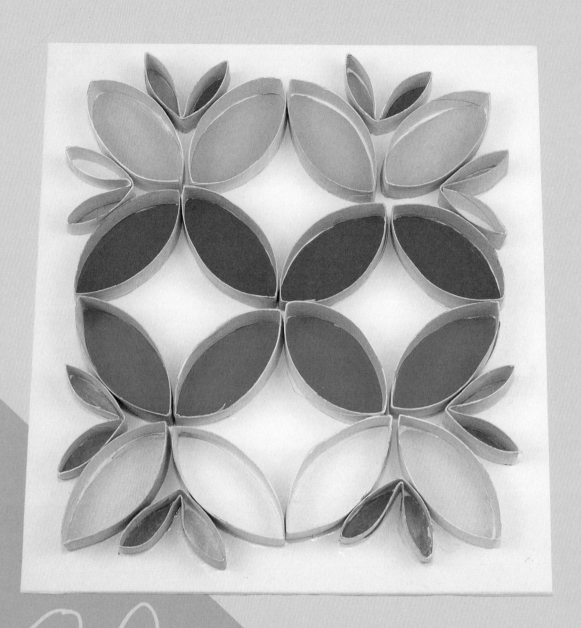

TRY A BLACK AND WHITE VERSION
FOR A DRAMATIC EFFECT.

2. To make the arrangement shown here, make 16 of the toilet-roll tube rings into leaf shapes by pinching them at opposite ends. Then make eight of the rings into bow shapes, by first making a leaf shape and then folding the whole piece in half.

4. Take the shapes off and paint each pencilled shape. You can follow the colours pictured or choose your own. Leave to dry completely.

3. Arrange the leaf and bow shapes on the foam board in the arrangement pictured or make any other pattern you want. Once you are happy, lightly trace around the inside of each shape with a pencil, so that you have a pencil outline of your design.

5. Glue the toilet-roll tube shapes on to the foam board in the same position. Leave to dry completely.

HANGING HEARTS

Using patterned paper brightens up this cute design.

TO MAKE ONE HEART HANGER YOU WILL NEED:

Paint in assorted colours

Paintbrush

6 toilet-roll tubes

Double-sided sticky tape

Scissors

Assorted patterned paper

Length of ribbon, about 80 cm

Hole punch

1. Choose three colours of paint and paint all six toilet-roll tubes on the inside only, making two tubes of each colour. Leave them to dry completely.

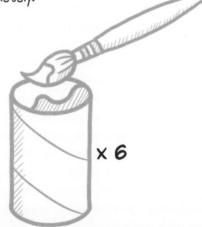

× 6

64

2. Stick a length of double-sided sticky tape down the side of each tube, and then stick another length down the opposite side.

3. Cover the tubes with the different styles of patterned paper. Roll the tubes in the paper so it sticks to the tape. Trim the paper to size if needed.

4. Cut each of the tubes into four equal-sized rings.

5. Shape each ring into a heart by first pinching opposite ends into points, to make a leaf shape, and then holding one point in one hand while you fold the top point inwards into a heart shape.

6. Putting one heart to one side, arrange the others into a large ring on a flat surface, but do not stick them together yet.

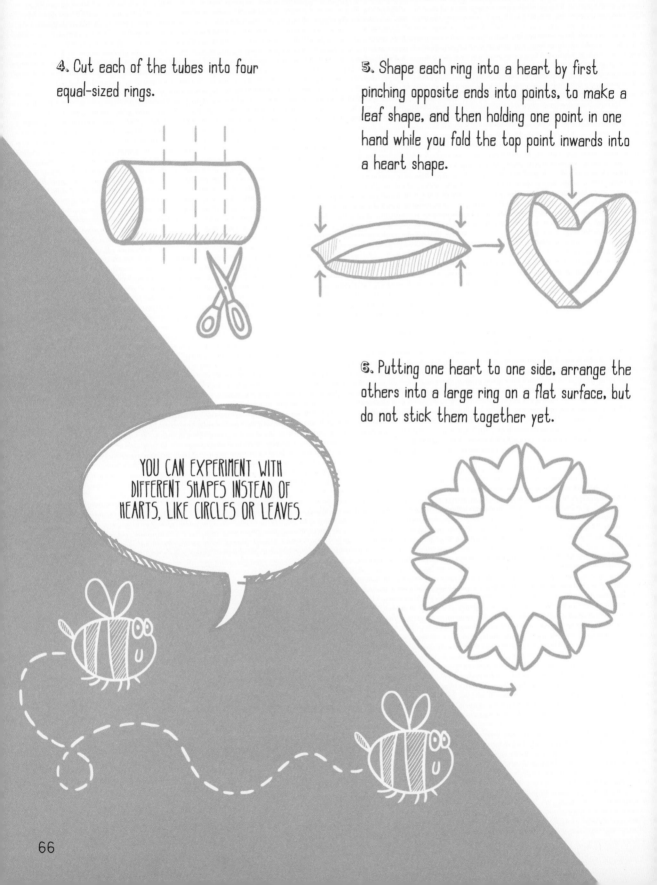

YOU CAN EXPERIMENT WITH DIFFERENT SHAPES INSTEAD OF HEARTS, LIKE CIRCLES OR LEAVES.

7. Take your ribbon and fold it in half to make a long loop. Lay this loop down lengthways across the heart ring, so it passes through the middle and between the top two and bottom two heart shapes. Secure the heart ring and ribbon together in this position using double-sided sticky tape.

8. Take the one heart you reserved in step 6 and squash it together so the two points meet. Create a hole through both points using a hole punch.

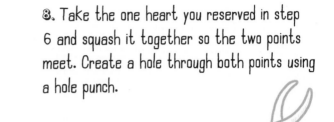

9. Feed the two loose ends of ribbon through these two holes, and push the heart shape up until it meets the ring. Tie the two loose ends of ribbon into a bow to secure it.

MINI VILLAGE

Why not get creative with the design of these little huts until you have a whole village?

TO MAKE TWO HUTS YOU WILL NEED:

1 toilet-roll tube

Scissors

Paints

Paintbrush

Black fine-line pen

Card, patterned or textured

Compass and pencil

Sticky tape

PVA glue

1. Cut the toilet-roll tube in half, so you have two rings.

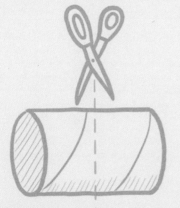

2. Take one half of the tube and paint the outside in a bright colour. Leave it to dry.

3. Take the other half of the toilet-roll tube and draw a house or cottage design on to one side. Include a door placed near the bottom edge.

5. To make the roofs, cut two circles, about 10 cm in diameter, from the card.

10 cm

4. Using scissors, cut around the door at the top, bottom and one side, so you can bend it open. Once the painted half of the toilet-roll tube is dry, cut a door into this piece too. Fold the doors on both huts outwards so they sit slightly open.

6. Using a pencil, lightly divide each circle into three equal-sized sections. Cut one of these sections out from each circle.

7. Curl each circle piece into a cone shape and secure with sticky tape.

8. Glue the roofs to the top of your huts.

USE A KITCHEN-ROLL TUBE TO MAKE A CASTLE TURRET.

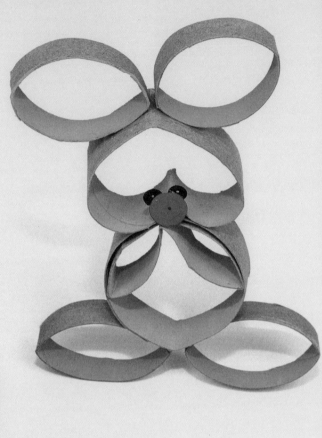

MINI MOUSE

Cute friends for your desk.

TO MAKE ONE MOUSE YOU WILL NEED:

1 toilet-roll tube

Pink paint

Paintbrush

Scissors

Double-sided sticky tape

Pencil

Mini pink pom pom

Black bead

PVA glue

1. Paint the toilet-roll tube pink on the inside. Leave to dry completely. Cut the tube into six 1 cm-wide rings. Keep the rest of the tube to one side.

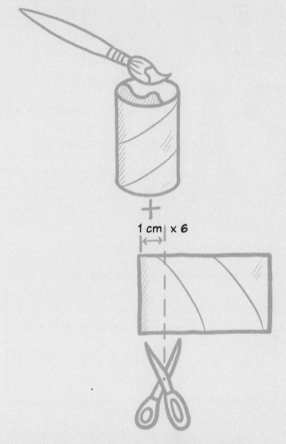

1 cm x 6

2. To make the body, take one ring and pinch it slightly at one end, then open it out to a circular shape again.

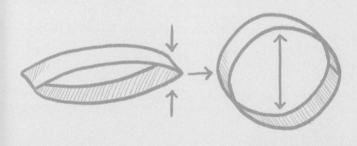

3. To make the feet, take another ring and pinch it closed at both ends, so it flattens. Secure it with tape at the middle point, so it stays flattened but makes a bow shape.

4. Tape the feet to the body at the pinched end of the body.

5. To make the paws, take another ring and pinch it closed at both ends, so it flattens. Then bring the pinched ends together, so the flattened ring folds in half. Tape the paws on to one side of the body.

6. To make the head, take another ring and pinch it slightly at both ends, then open it out to a circular shape again.

7. Tape the head on top of the body. Imagine one of the pinched points is the mouse's nose, and tape the head so it's slightly pointing up.

8. Take another ring and tape it to one side of the head for an ear. To make the other ear, take the last ring and pinch it slightly at both ends to make a leaf shape. Tape this next to the first ear, on the side that is nearer the top of the head.

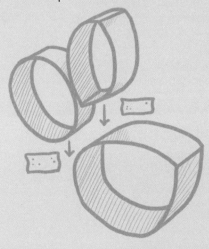

9. To make the tail, cut a 0.5 cm-wide ring from the leftover piece of toilet-roll tube, then cut the ring to break the circle. To make the strip into a tail, curl it in a spiral around a pencil.

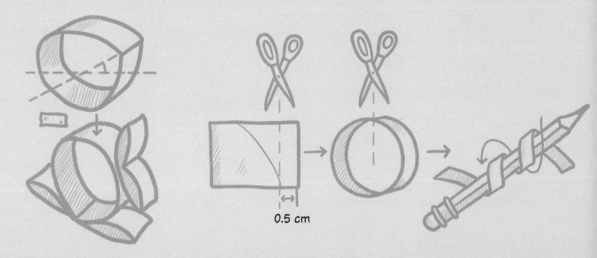

0.5 cm

10. Tape the tail to the base of the mouse's body, on the opposite side to the paws.

11. To give the mouse features, glue the mini pom pom to the tip of its nose and the black bead to the top of its head for an eye.

YOU CAN MAKE A BUNNY INSTEAD BY MAKING A HEART-SHAPED HEAD THAT LOOK LIKE CHEEKS, AND DIFFERENT-SHAPED EARS AND BIGGER FEET.

SUPER SEEDLINGS

Toilet-roll tubes are the perfect-sized pot to grow your own tiny seedlings.

TO MAKE ONE SEEDLING POT YOU WILL NEED:

Scissors
Waxed or greaseproof paper
1 toilet-roll tube
String
Soil
A little water
Seeds, such as basil

1. Using scissors, cut a square of waxed or greaseproof paper, with each side of the square three times the length of your toilet-roll tube.

2. Place the tube in the centre of the square of paper and gather the sides and corners of the paper around it.

3. Secure the paper around the tube by tying a length of string around the middle. If the paper looks too tall, you should tear off a little at the top to allow your seeds more light.

4. Fill the toilet-roll tube almost to the top with soil. Flatten the surface with your fingers.

5. Moisten the soil with a little water. Sprinkle a small pinch of seeds in the middle of the soil.

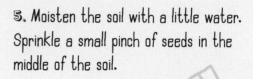

6. Cover the seeds with a fine layer of soil. Using your fingers, firm down the soil over the seeds.

7. To make sure your seeds will grow happily, follow the growing instructions on the back of the seed packet.

READ THE PLANTING INSTRUCTIONS ON THE BACK OF YOUR SEED PACKET FIRST. DIFFERENT SEEDS NEED PLANTING IN DIFFERENT WAYS.

ADVENT CALENDAR

The most exciting way to count down to Christmas.

TO MAKE ONE CALENDAR YOU WILL NEED:

12 toilet-roll tubes

Scissors

Zigzag scissors

PVA glue

Clothes pegs

Picture frame, with glass removed, at least 29 cm x 35 cm in size

Patterned wrapping paper, large enough to cover the backboard of the picture frame

Sticky tape

5 lengths of ribbon, longer than the width of the picture frame

24 mini pegs or paperclips

24 small toys or sweets

1. Cut each of the 12 toilet-roll tubes in half, and then cut one end of each piece with the zigzag scissors to make a decorative edge.

2. To turn each piece into a pocket, glue the straight-cut ends of each piece closed. You can use pegs to hold them closed while the glue dries. Leave to dry completely.

3. Remove the backboard from the picture frame.

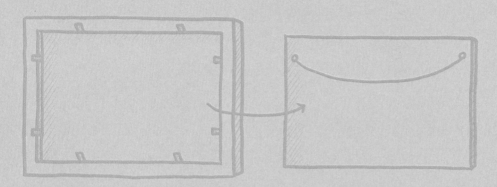

4. Cover the backboard with patterned wrapping paper, securing it at the back with sticky tape.

5. Add five lengths of ribbon, running parallel, horizontally across the backboard. Secure them by gluing the ends around the back of the backboard.

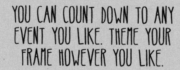

YOU CAN COUNT DOWN TO ANY EVENT YOU LIKE. THEME YOUR FRAME HOWEVER YOU LIKE.

6. Place the backboard back into the picture frame wih the rows of ribbon facing outwards. You can secure it at the back with sticky tape around the edges.

8. Place small toys or sweets in each pocket.

7. Draw the numbers 1 to 24 on the pockets. Then, using mini pegs or paperclips, attach them in order across the ribbons in the frame, five to each row and four on the last.

DANCING BUTTERFLY

Creating these intricate swirls takes some practice, but the effect is stunning.

1. Take one toilet-roll tube and paint it a colour of your choice, on the outside only. Leave to dry completely, then flatten the tube and cut off four 1.5 cm-wide rings and one 0.5 cm-wide ring.

TO MAKE ONE BUTTERFLY YOU WILL NEED:

2 toilet-roll tubes
Paint in assorted colours
Paintbrush
Scissors
Double-sided sticky tape
Length of ribbon, about 20 cm long
A pencil
PVA glue

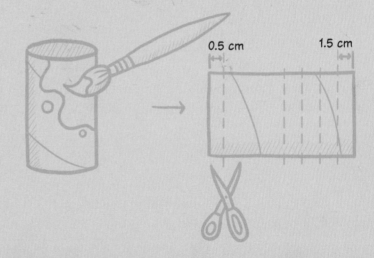

0.5 cm   1.5 cm

2. Take the four 1.5 cm-wide rings and make one of them smaller by cutting it at one of the folded creases to break the ring, cutting off a 1 cm strip from the end and then taping it back into shape using double-sided sticky tape. Repeat this with one other ring, so you have two large rings and two smaller ones.

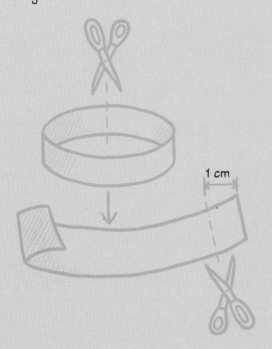

3. Arrange the four pieces into a butterfly shape, with the two larger pieces above the two smaller ones. Insert the end of the length of ribbon between the two larger pieces and secure everything together with double-sided sticky tape.

4. To make the butterfly's antennae, take the 0.5 cm-wide ring and separate it into two, equal-sized strips.

6. Take the other toilet-roll tube and cut it into three equal-sized rings. Paint each ring a different colour, inside and out, and leave to dry completely.

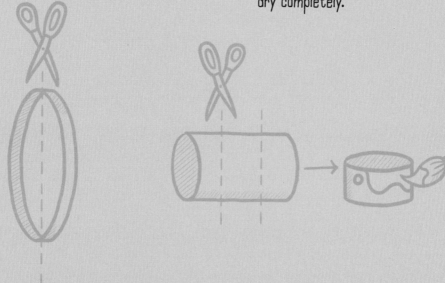

5. Wrap one end of each strip around a pencil to give them slight curls. Glue these antennae pieces, curls facing outwards, to the top middle of the butterfly, where the ribbon is inserted.

7. Flatten all three of the painted pieces and again cut each of them into 0.5-cm-wide rings. Make a cut into each ring to break the circles.

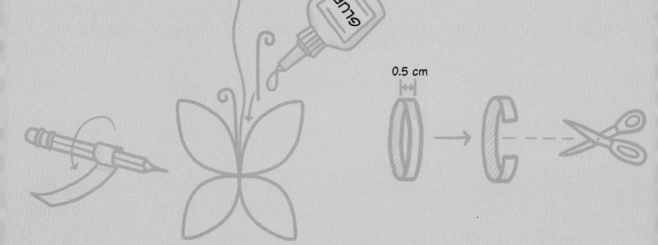

0.5 cm

8. Form the strips into different decorative pieces by following the instructions below. All the decorative pieces should be small enough to fit inside the butterfly wing pieces, so you may have to trim the strips to size with scissors.

a. Make a curl by wrapping a strip tightly around a pencil.

b. Make a leaf by taping a strip into a small circle and then pinching the circle at opposite ends to make points.

c. Make a spiral by rolling a strip tightly around itself using your thumb and forefinger.

9. Arrange the decorative pieces you have made inside the wings of the butterfly, making the two sides symmetrical. Secure the pieces with glue and leave to dry completely before hanging.

GLUE

EXPERIMENT BY MAKING DIFFERENT STYLES OF DECORATIVE PIECES. YOU COULD MAKE ZIGZAGS BY FOLDING A STRIP OF TOILET-ROLL TUBE BACKWARDS AND FORWARDS.

GLITTER SPIRALS

Even toilet-roll tubes can have glitz and glam.

TO MAKE ONE SPIRAL YOU WILL NEED:

Paint

Metallic paint

Paintbrush

1 toilet-roll tube

Scissors

Sequins

PVA glue

Safety pin

A length of elastic thread, about 30 cm

1. Paint the toilet-roll tube a bright colour on the inside and with metallic paint on the outside. Leave to dry completely.

2. Cut eight diagonal slits from top to bottom around the tube, about 1 cm from the top and bottom edges. Because the tube is curved, the diagonal slits will look like they are spiralling around the roll.

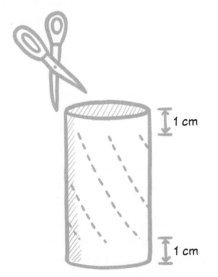

3. Gently squash the lantern at both ends to make the strips bulge out around the middle slightly.

4. To add some more sparkle, glue sequins around the top, bottom and middle of the tube. Leave to dry completely.

5. Using a safety pin, poke two holes at opposite sides, about 0.5 cm from the top edge of the tube. Tie a loop of elastic thread through the holes so you can hang up the glitter spiral.

0.5 cm

IF YOU CAN'T FIND METALLIC PAINT, JUST USE COLOURFUL PAINT INSTEAD AND ADD EVEN MORE SEQUINS.

LITTLE FIR TREE

A little fir tree – perfect for festive cheer.

TO MAKE ONE TREE YOU WILL NEED:
10 toilet-roll tubes (extra if needed)
Scissors
Double-sided sticky tape
PVA glue

1. Cut eight toilet-roll tubes into 1.5 cm-wide rings.

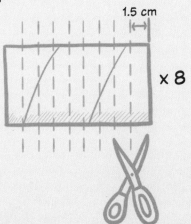

1.5 cm

× 8

2. Put five rings to one side, then make half the remaining rings into leaf shapes by pinching them at opposite ends.

3. Make the other half of the rings into heart shapes, by first making a leaf shape and then holding one point in one hand while you fold the top point inwards into a heart shape.

5. To make the next level up, repeat this, but this time stick nine heart shapes into a circle. Repeat this with alternating leaf and heart shapes, using one less piece each time to gradually make the layers smaller. You should make five layers in total.

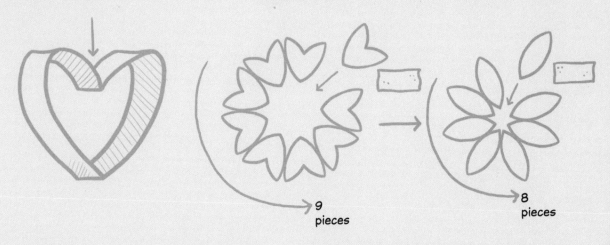

9
pieces

8
pieces

4. To make the base of the tree, stick 10 leaf shapes together side by side to create a circle, using double-sided sticky tape.

6. To build the tree, glue the layers on top of each other, starting with the biggest and ending with the smallest.

10
pieces

GLUE

7. To make the top piece, take the five rings that you reserved in step 2, and fold them all into bow shapes. Make a bow shape by first making a leaf shape and then folding the whole piece in half.

8. Using double-sided sticky tape, stick four of the bow shapes together side by side to create a circle, in the same way you created each layer.

9. Glue the bow ring on the top of your tree and then finish it by gluing the final bow at the very top.

BUILD A MEGA TREE USING AS MANY LAYERS AS YOU LIKE.

MATERIALS CHECK LIST

You'll find a list of everything you need on the first page of each project, but below is a list of the materials that are used very frequently.

- Toilet-roll tubes
- A4 paper – coloured, patterned and plain
- Cardboard – coloured, textured and plain
- Wrapping paper – patterned
- Pencils
- Pens – black felt-tips and fine-liners
- Paints
- Paintbrushes
- Scissors
- Sticky tape
- Double-sided sticky tape

- PVA glue
- Ribbon
- String

INDEX

First published in Great Britain in 2015 by Buster Books, an imprint of Michael O'Mara Books Limited,
9 Lion Yard, Tremadoc Road, London SW4 7NQ

Copyright © Buster Books 2015

W www.busterbooks.co.uk   f Buster Children's Books   @BusterBooks

ISBN: 978-1-78055-338-2

2 4 6 8 10 9 7 5 3 1

This book was printed in June 2015 by Leo Paper Products Ltd, Heshan Astros Printing Limited,
Xuantan Temple Industrial Zone, Gulao Town, Heshan City, Guangdong Province, China.